Nebraska

Nebraska

a photographic celebration

AMERICAN & WORLD GEOGRAPHIC PUBLISHING

Printed in Korea by Sung In Printing, San Mateo, California

Above: Deserted homestead south of Chadron. LARRY MAYER
Left: Knox County farmer Jim Wagner takes a break from
work. JAMES JAVORSKY

Half-title page: Silver maples dressed in early autumn finery
line the banks of Maple Creek near Fremont. GLENN VAN
NIMWEGEN

Title page: Dead trees etched in silver stand in stark contrast
against Calamus Reservoir near Burwell. LARRY MAYER

Indian Cave at Indian Cave State Park, located in scenic southeastern
Nemaha County along the Missouri River. STEVE MULLIGAN

White-tailed fawn hidden among the lush foliage of 1,250-acre Fontenelle Forest Nature Center near Bellevue.
MARK DIETZ

Sunlight dances on the petals of beeplants in the Fort Niobrara National Wildlife Refuge near Valentine. GLENN VAN NIMWEGEN

Historic landmark Scotts Bluff National Monument on the Oregon Trail. LARRY MAYER

The namesake spire of Chimney Rock National Historic Site. LARRY MAYER

Collage of fall colors along the Missouri River near Omaha. LARRY MAYER

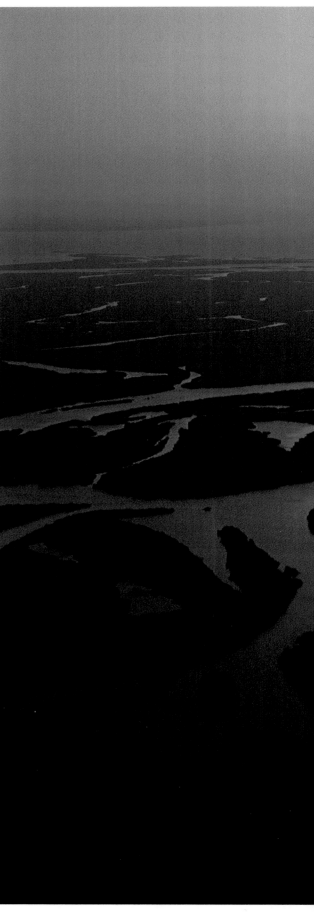

Above: State Capitol in Lincoln. LARRY MAYER

Right: Sunrise over the Missouri River at the upper end of Lewis and Clark Lake in northeastern Nebraska. LARRY MAYER

The railyard at southeastern Plattsmouth serves transport for a wide variety of agricultural and manufactured goods crossing the country. LARRY MAYER

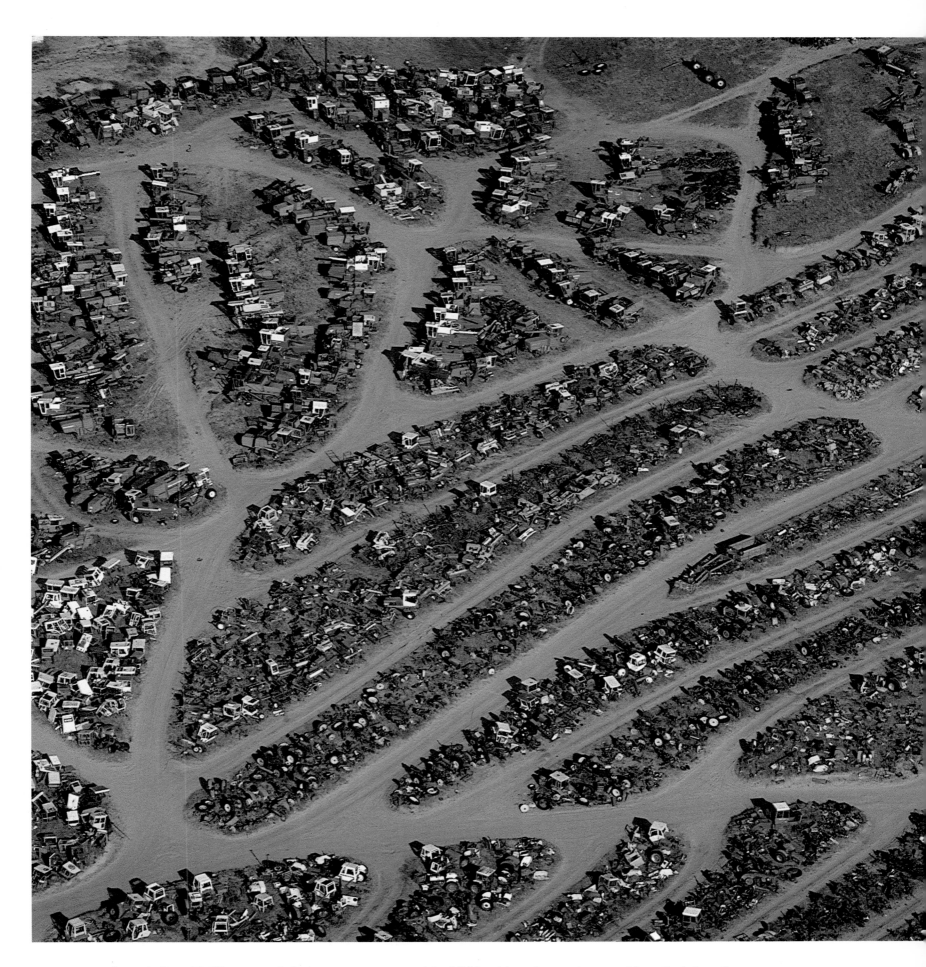

Joan & Gary Phillips started their tractor graveyard in 1966 with only one tractor. Now their location at Northport spans eighty acres. LARRY MAYER

A main tributary of the Missouri River, the Niobrara River flows along the northern edge of Nebraska's sandhills. MATT BRADLEY

Right: Massive trees draped with ivy form a leafy tunnel over a country road near Gretna.

JOE JENSEN

Above: A fisherman patiently waits at 43,000-acre Lake McConaughy on the North Platte River. RON SPOMER.
Overleaf: Lifting off at DeSoto National Wildlife Refuge, a flock of snow geese continue their fall migration.
P. MICHAEL WHYE

The unusual formations of Toadstool Park, nestled in the Oglala National Grasslands, are silhouetted in shades of violet. GLENN VAN NIMWEGEN

Left: Morning in late summer at majestic Scotts Bluff National Monument, with Dome Rock on the left and Crown Rock on the right. JEFF GNASS

Below: White-tail deer pause to survey their surroundings at the Fontenelle Forest Nature Center near Bellevue. MARK DIETZ

Sandhill cranes, *Grus canadensis*, settle down for the evening on the North Platte River near Kearney. GLENN VAN NIMWEGEN

Threading its way through the Gene Leahy Mall in metropolitan downtown Omaha, a man-made lagoon reflects the soft lights of evening. JAMES BLANK

Geometric designs near the town of Winnebago on the Winnebago Indian Reservation. LARRY MAYER

Decorated with thick hoarfrost, trees from Camp Brewster overlook the Missouri River in southeastern Sarpy County. MARK DIETZ

December snowfall on a pasture in Knox County. JAMES JAVORSKY

Muskrats sleep snug in winter sandhills of
western Nebraska. GLENN VAN NIMWEGEN

Above: Immature hawk rests on the branches of a tree on the 4-D Ranch in Garden County. MARK DIETZ

Left: A fish-eating bald eagle, *Haliaeetus leucocephalus*, can grow to a length of two-and-a-half feet and have a wingspread of seven-and-half feet. STEPHEN & MICHELE VAUGHAN

Frosted pines line the banks of Snake Falls on the Snake River in northern Cherry County. STEVE MULLIGAN

University Hill, located on the 2,700-acre Agate Fossil Beds National Monument, yields fossils formed about nineteen million years ago. KENT & DONNA DANNEN

Spectacular lightning strikes illuminate the horizon in Sioux County. JAMES JAVORSKY

A rain shower moves across the expansive sandhills of Cherry County.
LARRY MAYER

A pastoral resting place west of Lincoln. LARRY MAYER

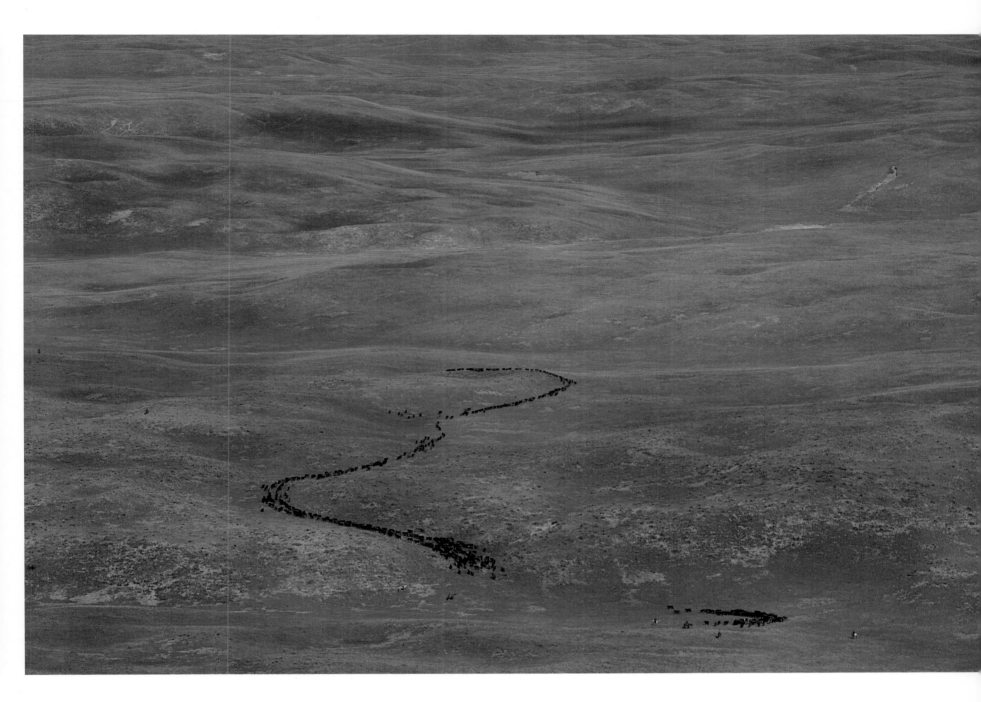

Cowboys drive cattle in the rolling sandhills of the Snake River country.

LARRY MAYER

Teaching his grandson how to hill a bean field in Douglas County. GARY TARLETON/BORLAND

Fertile Nebraska farmland stretches out westward from Lincoln. LARRY MAYER

Above: Native Nebraska grasses and a variety of agates are found in the 94,334-acre Oglala National Grasslands, named for the Oglala Tribe of the Dakota Sioux. TOM BEAN

Facing page: A well-kept farm near Crete. LARRY MAYER

Facing page: Freshly planted fields and a Nebraska farm near Humbolt form agricultural mosaic. LARRY MAYER

Silt deposit designs at the confluence of the Missouri and Niobrara rivers. LARRY MAYER

Top: First Presbyterian Church in Bellevue, built in 1856, stands as an enduring testament of the early Nebraska pioneers' faith. P. MICHAEL WHYE
Facing page: Two Brothers statue at Boys Town symbolizes the motto "He ain't heavy, Father, he's m'brother." FATHER FLANAGAN'S BOYS' HOME
Overleaf: Cumulonimbus clouds build over eastern Nebraska. JERRY GILDEMEISTER

Facing page: Deer cross the blue waters of the Niobrara River near Valentine. LARRY MAYER

Dismal River and Nebraska National Forest. LARRY MAYER

Named for trapper Hiram Scott, who died near the bluffs around 1828, Scotts Bluff National Monument towers 800 feet above the North Platte River. LARRY MAYER

Early sunrise along the North Loup River in central Nebraska.

GLENN VAN NIMWEGEN

Aptly nicknamed the Cornhusker State, Nebraska lists corn as its most important field crop.

JAMES BLANK

Knox County farmer near Bloomfield makes hay while the sun shines. JAMES JAVORSKY

Lush farmland spreading out from the Elkhorn River near Stanton. LARRY MAYER

Above: The eroded badlands north of Crawford in Toadstool Park. LARRY MAYER

Facing page: Redfern Table in the sprawling hills northwest of Lexington. LARRY MAYER

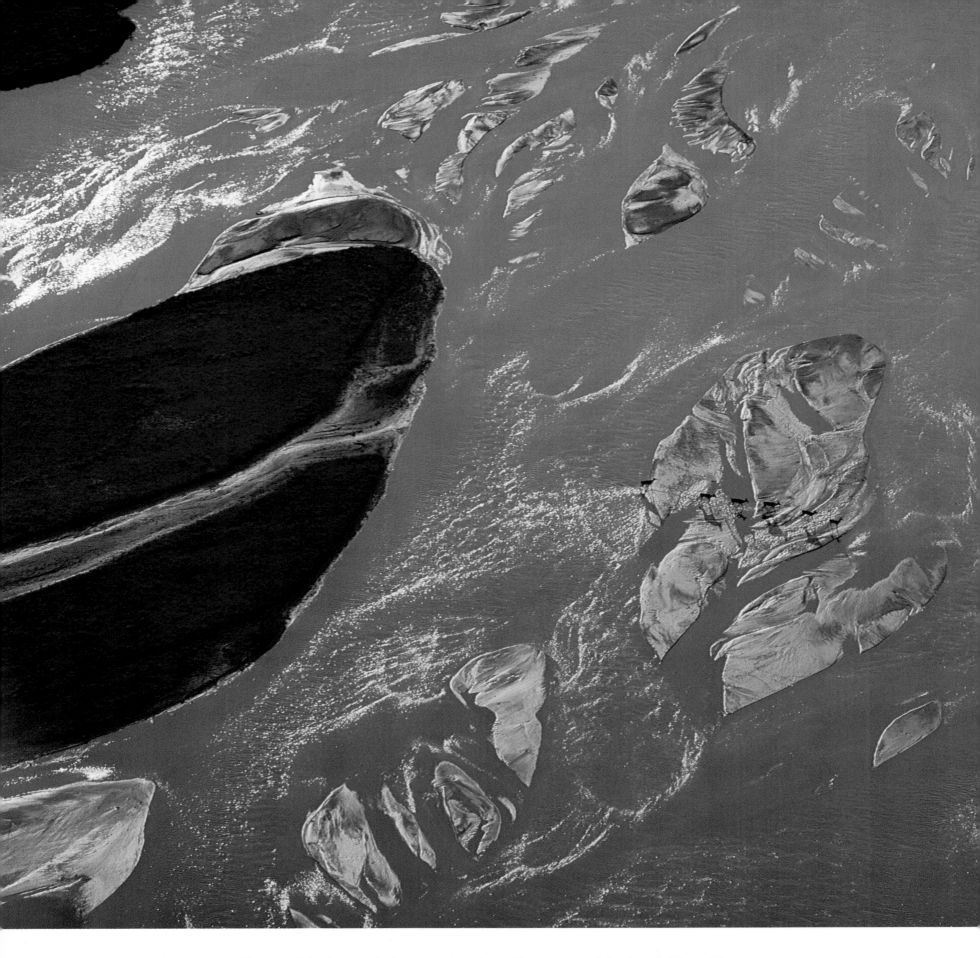

They look both ways before crossing the swift currents of the North Platte River. LARRY MAYER

Off the shore of Lewis and Clark Lake near Niobrara. LARRY MAYER

Strip farming patterns create country-quilt effect near Alliance. LARRY MAYER

Cumulus, or fair weather clouds, float above the many lakes of the
Valentine National Wildlife Refuge. LARRY MAYER

Left: Sunrise breaks over the Niobrara River. LARRY MAYER

Below: A red fox, genus *Vulpes*, pauses in the snow of western Nebraska. W. PERRY CONWAY

Bottom: A cool breeze coming off the Snake River Falls, southwest of Valentine, refreshes northern sandhill visitors. P. MICHAEL WHYE

Facing page: Rails of gold in an early sunrise over Minden in Kearney County. TOM COKER

Early on a Memorial Day, David Jundt of Creighton joins in honoring the fallen dead. JAMES JAVORSKY

Above: Springtime in the sandhills near Hyannis in western Nebraska. LARRY MAYER

Left: The rain falls gently on the plains next to Lake Minatare in the North Platte National Wildlife Refuge. LARRY MAYER

Patrons belly up to the water in Harlan County Lake near Alma. LARRY MAYER

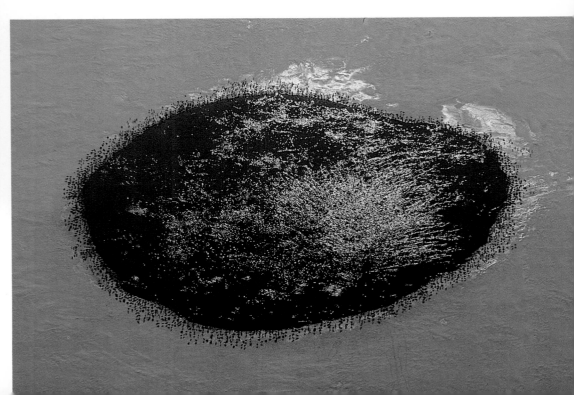

Cornhusker fever at the University of Nebraska, Memorial Stadium. NEBRASKA
DEPARTMENT OF ECONOMIC DEVELOPMENT–DIVISION OF TRAVEL & TOURISM

The band plays at University of Nebraska Memorial
Stadium in Lincoln. MICHAEL MASSEY/UNICORN

Cheyenne County is one of Nebraska's largest wheat-producing counties. LARRY MAYER

Country road takes me home to Garden County. TOM BEAN

Overleaf: Life-giving sun rises above Lewis and Clark Lake in northeastern Nebraska. LARRY MAYER

Cattle feedlot operation near Omaha. LARRY MAYER

Awaiting Harrison's livestock sale. LARRY MAYER

Mushroom and grasses at 12 Mile Camp on the Niobrara River. STEVE MULLIGAN

Silver maples line the banks of Cub Creek at Homestead National Monument near Beatrice. GLENN VAN NIMWEGEN

A raccoon, *Procyon lotor*, sits tucked inside a cottonwood log. W. PERRY CONWAY

Facing page: Blooming yucca below Eagle Rock at Scotts Bluff National Monument. RON SPOMER

Strip farming meets the bluffs near McGrew on the North Platte River.
LARRY MAYER

Sunset closes the chapter of another day on snow-covered farmland southwest of Lincoln. LARRY MAYER

Omaha in winter. LARRY MAYER

A pronghorn rests among the tall grasses of western Nebraska. D. DVORAK, JR.

Ruts from the Oregon Trail are still visible in Ash Hollow State Historical Park. GLENN VAN NIMWEGEN

74

A solitary Oregon Trail stone marker sits inside
Ash Hollow State Historical Park, posting the trail
hopeful emigrants followed westward. TOM TILL

Rosenblatt Stadium hosts the annual NCAA College Baseball World Series, as well as the Omaha Royals, the AAA farm club of the Kansas City Royals. GREATER OMAHA CONVENTION & VISITORS BUREAU.

Farm Aid III at Memorial Stadium in Lincoln. RANDY HAMPTON

Above: Winter corn harvest near Sutherland. LARRY MAYER

Facing page: Sectioned land west of Lincoln. LARRY MAYER

Above: Looking out towards the North Platte River and valley floor from Scotts Bluff National Monument. CHARLIE BORLAND

Left: Cliffs of the Scotts Bluff National Monument are composed of Arikaree sandstone, siltstone and volcanic ash. TOM TILL

81

Facing page: Downtown Omaha. LARRY MAYER

Above the capital city. LARRY MAYER

Facing page: Smith Falls in Cherry County. STEVE MULLIGAN

Columbine and basswood at Indian Cave State Park in Nemaha County.
STEVE MULLIGAN

Facing page: "And God saw [the Niobrara River] that he had made and behold it was very good" (Genesis 1:31). LARRY MAYER

The glow of sunset transforms the North Platte River into threads of silver. LARRY MAYER

James Reinders built Carhenge in 1987 during a family reunion, his whimsical idea coming after a visit to Stonehenge in England. Located in a field north of Alliance, it is now maintained by Friends of Carhenge. LARRY MAYER

Reeds along the North Platte River in the Sandy Channel State Recreation Area near Kearney. TOM TILL

90

Celebrating their Native American heritage with dance and music, competitors at Santee Indian Reservation powwow wear elaborate feather bustles. JAMES JAVORSKY

Facing page: Monday's chores in Saline County. LARRY JAVORSKY

A long–billed avocet, *Recurvirostra americana*, found in Nebraska marshes and fresh waterways, looks for a dinner of crustaceans. W. PERRY CONWAY

Merritt Reservoir State Recreation Area. LARRY MAYER

Facing page: Sandhills ranch south of Valentine. LARRY MAYER

Center pivot irrigation systems encircle feedlot near Broadwater. LARRY MAYER

An elegant male wood duck, *Aix sponsa,* enjoys a warm afternoon.

Misty morning shadows on South Loup River near Broken Bow. GLENN VAN NIMWEGEN

Deep purple falls over North Loup River. LARRY MAYER

Above: Hot chocolate topped with marshmallows waits in the warming house for ice skaters. LARRY MAYER

Below: Shoppers in downtown Omaha hurry home to dinner. P. MICHAEL WHYE

Right: With three districts totalling 257,360 acres of evergreens, the Nebraska National Forest offers recreationists pristine choices. LARRY MAYER

Below: Pine trees release a storm of pollen in Nebraska National Forest near Dunning. LARRY MAYER

Below: The Missouri River delineates the border between Nebraska and Iowa. LARRY MAYER

Above: Jail Rock warned pilgrims on the Oregon and Mormon trails of the challenging mountainous terrain lying ahead. GLENN VAN NIMWEGEN

Top: Between 1842 and 1860, three hundred thousand emigrants streamed past Courthouse Rock and Jail Rock. GLENN VAN NIMWEGEN

Left: Warm autumn breezes at Courthouse Rock still echo haunting sounds of people, wagons and livestock passing through on the Oregon and Mormon trails. GLENN VAN NIMWEGEN

"The Sower," a thirty-two-and-a-half foot bronze statue, proudly stands atop the ornate capitol dome in Lincoln. RANDY HAMPTON

One of the largest Czech settlements in the state, Wilber hosts the annual Czech Festival in August. P. MICHAEL WHYE

Sunflowers near Beatrice produce oil, seeds and fodder for livestock. CHARLIE BORLAND

Sit back, relax and enjoy the view at Platte River State Park north of Louisville.

RANDY HAMPTON

Crops and groves of trees blanket the earth in green near Winnebago.

LARRY MAYER

Above: Rugged buttes and canyons surrounding Pine Ridge in Chadron State Park—one small corner of the vast Louisiana Purchase. TOM TILL

Facing page: Wild indigo blooms among the sage in Toadstool Park. STEVE MULLIGAN

On their migratory journey south to Texas and Mexico, long-legged sandhill cranes rest at Rowe Sanctuary near Kearney. GLENN VAN NIMWEGEN

All dressed up and ready for dinner, these hopeful sandhill cranes thrive on spilled grain. MARK DIETZ

Lazy summer afternoon at Gallagher Canyon Recreation area south of Cozad. CHARLIE BORLAND

Crescent Lake National Wildlife Refuge in Garden County.
BOB FIRTH

Drama in pastel near Crawford. LARRY MAYER

The irrigated countryside around Scottsbluff yields
large harvests of sugar beets. LARRY MAYER

Above: Berry-eating cedar waxwing, *Bombycilla cedrorum*. MARK DIETZ

Facing page: A white Christmas comes true for farmers outside Omaha. LARRY MAYER

Last page: Weather systems often collide over Nebraska, producing severe
thunderstorms of hail, high winds and tornadoes. W. PERRY CONWAY